FRED RAMEN

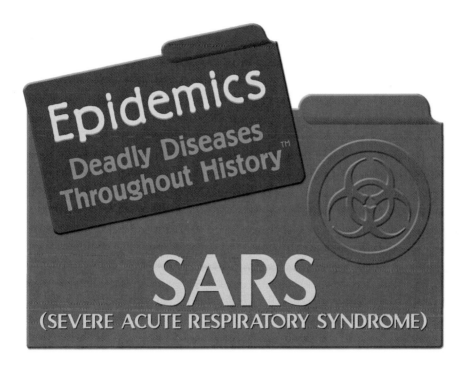

Epidemics
Deadly Diseases
Throughout History ™

SARS
(SEVERE ACUTE RESPIRATORY SYNDROME)

The Rosen Publishing Group, Inc.
New York

Published in 2005 by The Rosen Publishing Group, Inc.
29 East 21st Street, New York, NY 10010

Library of Congress Cataloging-in-Publication Data

Ramen, Fred.
SARS: severe acute respiratory syndrome/by Fred Ramen.—1st ed.
    p. cm.—(Epidemics)
Includes bibliographical references and index.
ISBN 1-4042-0258-7 (library binding)
1. SARS (Disease)—History—Juvenile literature.
I. Title. II. Series.
RA644.S17R35 2005
614.5′92—dc22

                                                2004017294

Manufactured in the United States of America

On the cover: A photomicrograph of lung tissue infected with SARS

CONTENTS

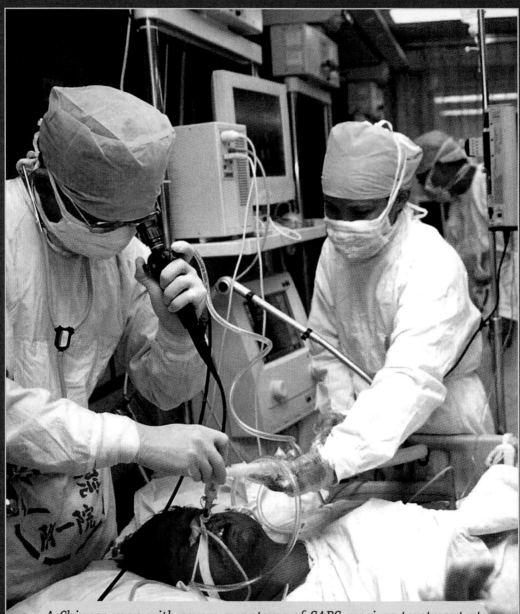

A Chinese man with severe symptoms of SARS receives treatment at a hospital in Guangzhou, on March 13, 2003. At the time, SARS had already infected more than 1,300 people.

INTRODUCTION

It was an ordinary occurrence during World War I (1914–1918) on what seemed to be another ordinary day—March 15, 1918. Just before breakfast, at the United States infantry training camp at Fort Riley, Kansas, a soldier reported to the base hospital. He had a sore throat, aches, and fever—classic symptoms of the flu.

It is not likely that the camp doctors thought much of his symptoms. Diseases and armies have always marched together. During the Civil War (1861–1865), for instance, far more men died from diseases such as typhus and dysentery than from gunshot wounds. Not until World War II (1939–1945) did combat wounds cause more deaths than diseases.

This is because war brings people together who would normally be apart. Young men from the country were thrown together with people from crowded cities. The people living in urban environments had been exposed to many different diseases while growing up and had developed immunities to them; the people from the countryside often had no such immunities. Because of this, it was common for soldiers in training to suddenly become sick.

The doctors, however, were worried about casualties of war. World War I was entering its fourth year in Europe. The United States had joined the side of the Allies (England, France, and other countries) in their fight against Germany and the Axis powers only a few months earlier, and almost no soldiers had crossed the ocean yet. But soon the doctors would realize something very different was happening, something new, unexpected, and deadly.

By noon on March 15, nearly 100 soldiers were sick. By the end of the week, almost 500 soldiers had come down with flulike symptoms. And worse, many had died of them.

The flu, or influenza, has always been a deadly disease. Each year it kills thousands of people around the world. But normally, influenza kills only young infants and children with underdeveloped immune systems or elderly people who have weakened immune systems and are less able to fight off disease. In 1918, the flu started to kill young adults in their twenties and thirties, people who normally have a higher resistance to disease.

The 1918 flu spread rapidly, first across the western United States and then into Europe, carried by the American soldiers now marching on the battle-fields of France. Along the way, it picked up a new name—the Spanish flu—because, at the time, it was believed to have first appeared in Spain. It spread through all the countries of Europe and then circled the world, killing thousands as it spread. In four years of nearly constant fighting, the armies of the world had killed some 9 million people while the

In this 1918 photo, nurses assist victims of the Spanish flu epidemic who have been moved outside in hopes that fresh air would help them.

Spanish flu killed at least 20 million. More Americans died of the flu than in any single war in U.S. history.

Then, just as suddenly as the Spanish flu emerged, it disappeared. Since 1920, there have been many flu epidemics, but none has been as deadly as the Spanish flu.

Meanwhile, enormous progress was made in all aspects of medicine. New drugs were developed that could cure diseases that had been killing humans for thousands of years. The deadly disease tuberculosis, for example, once a common illness of people living in crowded cities, was considerably weakened with the aid of drugs developed after World War II. Smallpox, one of the deadliest diseases in human history—an infection that had killed millions of Native Americans—was completely eradicated in the 1970s. Even polio, the crippling disease that caused paralysis without warning and had left President Franklin Delano Roosevelt unable to walk, could now be prevented with a simple vaccine. For a long time, it seemed that humans had finally conquered their ancient foes.

In the 1970s and early 1980s, a new disease called AIDS, or acquired immunodeficiency syndrome, rapidly spread around the world, killing people even in wealthy countries such as the United States. In poverty-stricken countries, the deadly virus devastated entire regions of the continent. As world travel became more common, strange, horrible diseases became a global threat.

Then, in November 2002, people began to get sick in China.

THE FIRST OUTBREAK

The Guangdong Province is located in south-eastern China, bordering the China Sea. Like Florida in the United States, it has a semitropical climate; temperatures rarely fall below 60° Fahrenheit (16° Celsius) and in the summer are usually around 80°F (27°C). Southeastern China has been inhabited by human beings for more than 100,000 years.

The capital of Guangdong, Guangzhou, or Canton, located on the Pearl River delta, has been in existence for almost 3,000 years and is currently home to 6.7 million people. It is a center of culture, art, and cuisine. One of the most important cities in China, Guangzhou has been a hub of commerce in southern Asia for centuries. In the last few decades, it has become home to new skyscrapers, hotels, and nightclubs. It is also no stranger to new diseases.

A History of Disease

In both 1957 and 1968, deadly kinds of influenza—the Asian flu and the Hong Kong flu—first appeared in Guangdong. Like many other regions of the developing world, the province is a place of extreme contrasts. Poor farmers live alongside wealthy businessmen. Modern airports and railroad stations are located just miles from rice paddies and open-air markets that date back thousands of years. In Guangdong Province, modern cities and their technology exist next to tiny isolated villages where people live their entire lives without traveling more than 20 miles (32 kilometers).

In November 2002, in the city of Foshan, 15 miles (24 km) south of Guangzhou, doctors began to see cases of a mysterious new illness. The sickness seemed to be an extreme form of pneumonia, but it spread more quickly and was not caused by any known pneumonia bacterium or virus.

The people who became sick seemed to have just another cold. But then their symptoms suddenly took a turn for the worse. Their temperatures shot up to over 100°F (38°C). Sometimes they experienced diarrhea. Often they developed a dry cough. Pneumonia—inflammation of the lungs, which prevents them from functioning properly—usually developed. Soon people with the disease could barely breathe; some had to be put on respirators, machines that breathed for them.

Unlike other respiratory illnesses, many people were dying from this new disease. The numbers were frightening: it seemed that almost one infected person in ten died. Many others became so sick that they nearly died.

The disease also seemed to spread rapidly, suddenly appearing in a new place. It seemed that some carriers were cap-

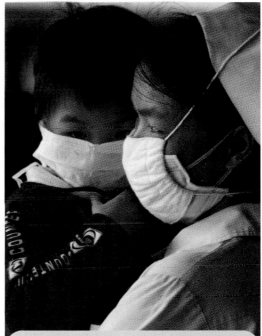

A Chinese nurse and a patient wear masks during the SARS epidemic in Guangzhou in March 2003.

able of infecting many people, while others did not spread the disease so rapidly. These "superspreaders" were infecting many people with the new illness, especially in hospitals throughout southern China.

Superspreaders

Although scientists have not yet identified the first case of the new illness—the so-called index patient, or the first person in a region to get a new disease— one of the first superspreaders has been identified.

He was a shrimp salesman from Foshan who became ill in February 2003. He checked into a hospital and was transferred twice, ending up in the Guangzhou Number Eight People's Hospital. Along the way, he had infected some ninety people, including many of his doctors. One of these doctors, a retired nephrologist (kidney doctor) named Liu Jianlun, would be responsible for spreading the disease even further.

Doctors in Guangdong were at a loss to explain the new illness. But they were severely limited in what they knew about it because of the actions of the Chinese government, which was trying to keep the growing problem quiet.

In early December 2002, the mysterious disease had spread to the city of Heyuan, about 120 miles (193 km) from Guangzhou. It spread from two patients admitted to a hospital there to its staff. Soon, more patients were coming down with the illness, and a panic began in the city. Drugstores were even running out of antibiotics, though they had not been shown to have any effect on the disease. Some people believed that breathing in fumes from vinegar would prevent them from getting the illness; soon vinegar had also vanished from store shelves.

Hiding the Truth

In response to the panic, the Chinese government issued a statement on January 3 saying that there was no epidemic in Heyuan. The panic stopped, but the disease kept spreading. However, the Chinese government kept information about the spread of the disease from the public. Officials prevented any news about the illness from being published in newspapers

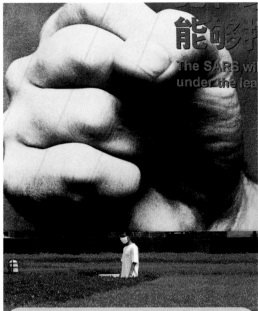

A man wearing a mask walks past a billboard during the 2003 SARS epidemic. The billboard reads, "SARS will surely be conquered by our government under the leadership of the Communist Party of China."

or broadcast on radio or television. This decision later proved tragic, because the people of Guangdong had no idea that the deadly disease was spreading through the region. This decision to keep things quiet also prevented doctors from taking appropriate steps to warn the public.

In the first days of the epidemic, however, there was little doctors could do except to isolate their patients. No known test worked to identify the new disease. Doctors were also unsure how it spread—was it transmitted by animals or spread by humans? No treatment seemed to work. Most people got sick and recovered. Some people got very sick and died, while others who seemed just as sick later recovered.

On January 28, 2003, the government sent a secret letter to the health care facilities of Guangdong Province. It described the symptoms of the new disease and explained that it was spreading to hospital workers. Government officials recommended keeping patients with the new pneumonia separated from the rest of the hospitals' patients because their coughing and mucus seemed to play an important role in spreading the illness. Officials said that the disease showed the characteristics of an epidemic. By this point, the shrimp salesman became known as the Poison King, because his coughing spread the disease to many people. He had already exposed medical workers in several hospitals throughout Guangzhou.

On February 11, 2003, the Chinese government briefly ended its media blackout. In a press conference held by health officials (with the permission of the local head of the Communist Party), the mystery disease was finally described, but the Chinese were told that its outbreak was under control. Shockingly,

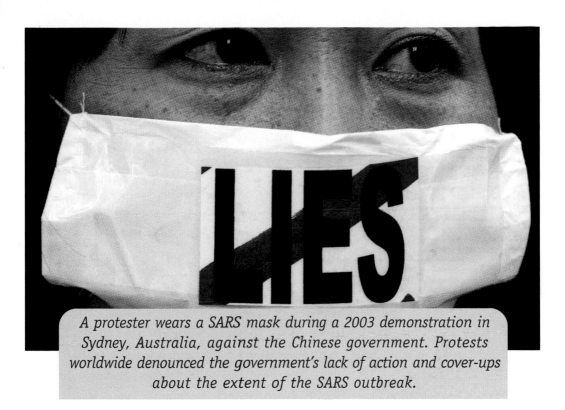

A protester wears a SARS mask during a 2003 demonstration in Sydney, Australia, against the Chinese government. Protests worldwide denounced the government's lack of action and cover-ups about the extent of the SARS outbreak.

it was revealed that 305 people had come down with the illness and eight of them had died. (We now know that the numbers were actually much higher and that the Chinese government did not accurately report them.) News of the illness and the press conference appeared in several Chinese newspapers. In response, the Chinese government, afraid of a massive panic among its citizens, started another news blackout that would last until March.

Dr. Liu Jianlun

Also in February, Dr. Liu Jianlun was treating the Poison King and forty-five others who had contracted the disease at the hospital. He was in contact with them every day, but was taking precautions to ensure that he didn't also get the disease. Dr. Liu felt healthy but a little tired from the heavy workload. Perhaps because of this, not long after the news conference, he decided to attend a family wedding in Hong Kong.

Dr. Liu started feeling ill as he and his family boarded a bus in Guangzhou on February 21. He had a fever, headache, and chills. That evening he checked into the Hotel Metropole in Hong Kong. He already had a bad cough and was feeling even worse than before.

By the next morning, the doctor knew what was wrong with him. He was too sick to go to the wedding. Instead, he managed to leave the hotel and walk to the nearby hospital in Kwong Wah.

"Lock me up," he told the staff there. "Don't touch me. I have contracted a virulent disease." It was too late—too late for Dr. Liu, and too late for Hong Kong.

A hygiene worker wearing a protective mask passes by the Hotel Metropole in Hong Kong, China, in March 2003. When Dr. Liu stayed at this hotel, he inadvertently helped spread SARS.

November 16, 2002

The first case of unusual pneumonia is reported in the Guangdong Province in southern China.

March 12, 2003

The World Health Organization (WHO) issues a global SARS alert.

March 17, 2003

An international network of eleven laboratories is established to research the cause of SARS. Fourteen suspected SARS cases are researched in the United States.

February 26, 2003

The first case of unusual pneumonia is reported in Hanoi, Vietnam.

February 28, 2003

Dr. Carlo Urbani examines an American businessman in a hospital in Hanoi.

March 15, 2003

SARS cases in Singapore and Canada are identified, and WHO issues yet another global alert about SARS symptoms and possible treatments. The Centers for Disease Control and Prevention (CDC) issues a travel advisory to various areas in Asia.

March 10, 2003

Dr. Urbani reports an outbreak of the strange respiratory illness, which he calls severe acute respiratory syndrome, or SARS. Twenty-two hospital workers are infected with the disease.

March 24, 2003

CDC officials believe that SARS is associated with a new strain of human coronavirus, which is the virus linked to the common cold.

March 29, 2003
Dr. Urbani dies of SARS.

April 3, 2003
A WHO team arrives in the Guangdong Province to investigate the SARS outbreak in China.

April 4, 2003
U.S. president George W. Bush adds SARS to the list of diseases to be quarantined.

April 9, 2003
The WHO identifies several superspreaders capable of spreading SARS to 100 persons or more.

April 16, 2003
The CDC confirms a new strain of the human coronavirus as the cause of SARS.

April 22, 2003
The CDC issues a health alert for all travelers to Toronto, Canada, which is the epicenter of the Canadian SARS outbreak.

April 28, 2003
Vietnam contains SARS successfully, and WHO removes Vietnam from the list of affected regions.

May 26, 2003
Canadian health officials report new SARS clusters of twenty-six probable and eight known SARS cases in four Toronto hospitals.

May 31–July 9, 2003
All WHO and CDC health alerts and travel advisories are lifted.

THE HONG KONG OUTBREAK

or three centuries, Europe and China have met at the island of Hong Kong, just off the southern coast of China. And here, for the first time, the mysterious disease of Guangdong would gain worldwide attention.

Archaeological excavations have shown that the Hong Kong region has been inhabited since the Stone Age—more than 6,000 years ago. Three hundred years ago, it was here that regular trade between the nations of Europe and China began. In 1841, after the first Opium War between Great Britain and China, Hong Kong was captured by the British and became a colony. At first, the British controlled only the island of Hong Kong and Kowloon, a part of the peninsula that juts out from the mainland. In 1898, however, it took out a ninety-nine-year lease on the rest of the peninsula from the Chinese, a region it named the New Territories.

Hong Kong became one of the most important British colonies outside of India. As the gateway to China's Pearl River, it was an important trading region. Its superb harbor also served as the crossroads of Southeast Asia, connecting the Indian and Pacific Oceans as well as trade routes from Malaysia and Indonesia. British investment in the colony made it one of the most modern areas in Asia.

However, the Chinese had never forgotten the loss of Hong Kong. In the 1980s, as the end of the lease on the New Territories approached, the government of the People's Republic of China let the British know that they would not renew the lease. The Chinese would not tolerate further British presence in the region, including Hong Kong proper. Years of negotiations finally resulted in a peaceful transition of power in 1997. Hong Kong officially became part of China, but the rights of its citizens—far greater than those of people living in China—were guaranteed. Hong Kong was also not required to adopt Communism, the official economic policy of China.

Island Epidemic

To a far greater degree than even Ghangzhou, Hong Kong was a modern region of China with superb doctors, a high standard of living, and technologically advanced hospitals. Yet, the former British colony was no stranger to epidemic diseases.

One of the worst influenza outbreaks of the twentieth century had passed through Hong Kong after emerging in Guangdong Province. In 1997, a new deadly form of influenza called either avian flu (because it first affected birds), or H5N1 (after the name of the influenza virus that caused the disease), struck Hong Kong. It infected eighteen people and killed six of them. A rapid response by the city's health care officials quickly contained the outbreak. City officials closed public parks and ordered the slaughter of more than 1.5 million chickens. The outbreak never became an epidemic. Doctors in Hong Kong were always on the lookout for new epidemics, especially an influenza outbreak. But by concentrating on influenza, they were actually slowed down in their response to the SARS epidemic, as the new disease was quite different from influenza.

Even before Dr. Liu Jianlun's arrival at Kwong Wah Hospital, rumors of a new outbreak of respiratory disease had reached Hong Kong. On February 11, text messages and phone calls from people in mainland China to relatives in Hong Kong had started a panic, much like the earlier one that had occurred in Heyuan.

Medical employees work in a laboratory researching the SARS virus in May 2003. The laboratory is in Hong Kong's Prince of Wales Hospital, which had suffered a severe SARS outbreak the previous April.

Further statements from the Chinese government and the World Health Organization (WHO), which had begun investigating the disease outbreak in Guangdong, revealed that the new disease was not the avian flu. In fact, on February 18, the Chinese government announced that chlamydia bacterium, a common cause of pneumonia, was the cause of the mysterious new disease. The January 28 memo issued by the Chinese government, which described the disease's symptoms in detail, was not released to Hong Kong health care authorities until after the epidemic began.

Created in 1948 by the United Nations, the World Health Organization (WHO) has been a leader in improving the health care of all the peoples of the world.

The WHO is currently made up of 192 member nations, including the United States. Each nation sends delegates to the World Health Assembly, the governing body of the WHO. The assembly elects the head of WHO, the director general. The current director general is Dr. Lee Jong-Wook.

One of the greatest accomplishments of the WHO was the eradication of smallpox. By developing a strategy of delivering smallpox vaccine immediately to areas where an outbreak of smallpox had occurred, the WHO's doctors and health care workers were able to contain the disease before it could start a new epidemic. As the number of vaccinated people grew, the disease became unable to infect new humans. In 1979, the WHO announced that smallpox, one of the most dreaded diseases in human history, had been eradicated. It currently survives only in a few laboratory samples.

The WHO continues to fight other infectious diseases with the goal of eradicating them as well. One of its current fights is to eliminate polio, which still afflicts people in many countries around the world. It also helps to coordinate international responses to epidemics, as it did during the SARS outbreak of 2003.

On February 13, a troubling case of pneumonia was discovered in Hong Kong. A thirty-three-year-old man was admitted to a hospital along with his wife and nine-year-old son. The family had recently traveled to

Fujian Province near Guangdong. Their youngest daughter had come down with severe pneumonia there and died on February 4. Although the man died on February 17, his wife and son recovered. Both the man and his son tested positive for a H5N1 infection, causing the WHO to issue a worldwide alert about influenza on February 19. Three days later, Dr. Liu arrived in Hong Kong and checked into the Metropole Hotel. Because of the false alarm caused by the avian flu–related deaths at the start of the outbreak, health care officials in Hong Kong were concentrating on the wrong disease.

The Mystery Unfolds

On February 22, the first two cases of the new disease appeared in Hong Kong. The first was Dr. Liu, who was admitted to Kwong Wah Hospital in Kowloon. The second was a forty-nine-year-old woman who had visited Henan Province in China at the end of January. She was admitted to Prince of Wales Hospital, where she was treated for severe pneumonia. She recovered quickly and did not seem to have spread the disease. But the next time Prince of Wales Hospital encountered the new disease, an epidemic would burst from inside its walls and into the city like an invisible bomb blast.

But Dr. Liu's visit to the city had already started an epidemic. In his short stay at the Hotel Metropole, he had infected several people. Each person would go on to start major outbreaks of the disease in several countries around the world. Epidemiologists later determined that 688 cases of the disease were directly linked to contact with Dr. Liu at the Hotel Metropole.

Spreading SARS

One of these cases was a twenty-six-year-old man who first began feeling ill on February 24. He was admitted to Prince of Wales Hospital on March 4. Although he was suffering from pneumonia, it was not as severe as other cases of the new disease. Because of this, doctors did not realize he was suffering from the mysterious disease from Guangdong, and the staff at Prince of Wales Hospital took no extra precautions while treating him. To help relieve his symptoms, they used a device called a nebulizer, which transforms liquid medicine into a fine mist, which is then fed through a breathing mask into the patient's airways. By using this device, the new disease spread much further around the hospital.

On March 10, 2003, the epidemic in Hong Kong officially began. On that day, eleven health care workers were forced to call in sick. They had come

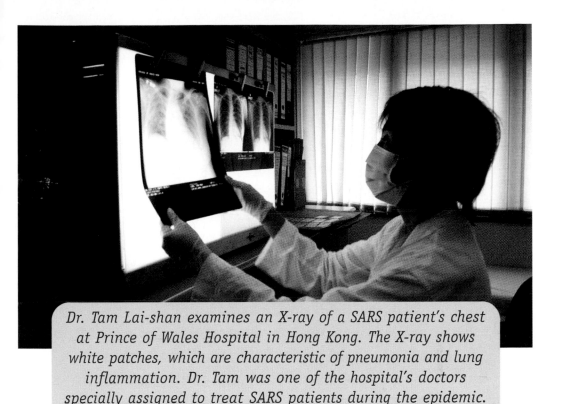

Dr. Tam Lai-shan examines an X-ray of a SARS patient's chest at Prince of Wales Hospital in Hong Kong. The X-ray shows white patches, which are characteristic of pneumonia and lung inflammation. Dr. Tam was one of the hospital's doctors specially assigned to treat SARS patients during the epidemic.

down with severe pneumonia, just like the people in Guangdong Province had—and, just like the outbreak there, the disease would spread from hospitals.

By the evening of March 12, more than fifty workers at Prince of Wales Hospital had come down with high fevers and chills. Half of these people were now patients at the hospital, and several of them were already showing signs of pneumonia. That day, the WHO issued its first alert about the new disease. The organization warned that there were outbreaks in China, Hong Kong, and Vietnam. The cause of the disease remained unknown, but the WHO again described the symptoms in detail so physicians around the world could be on alert.

By Friday, March 14, outbreaks had been identified at both Prince of Wales Hospital and Pamela Youde Nethersole Eastern Hospital, where six staff members had come down with the disease. There was also a patient at Princess Margaret Hospital who had been transferred from French Hospital in Hanoi, Vietnam. He seemed not only to have the disease, but to be the source of the outbreak in Vietnam.

On March 15, the WHO made a rare announcement. The international organization issued an emergency travel advisory indicating that the still unnamed disease had been observed in Canada, China, Hong Kong, Indonesia, the Philippines, Singapore, Thailand, and Vietnam. It alerted travelers around the world to the symptoms of the disease and finally gave it a name. Coined by Dr. Carlo Urbani, a WHO physician in Hanoi, the mysterious illness then became known as severe acute respiratory syndrome, or SARS.

The Hong Kong government had also taken steps to restrict the spread of the disease. All non-emergency admissions to the hospital were stopped, and by March 19, Prince of Wales Hospital stopped taking any more patients. Visiting rights were also suspended, causing much agony to relatives of sick people.

Dr. Carlo Urbani was the man who first described SARS to the world and gave the disease its name. His quick thinking and early action helped contain the Vietnam outbreak. Tragically, he was also one of the disease's victims.

Dr. Urbani was a specialist in parasitic diseases. He had dedicated his life to helping fight infectious diseases such as malaria, tuberculosis, and HIV infection and AIDS around the world. He was a member of the international organization Doctors Without Borders (also known by its French name, Médecins Sans Frontières). In 1999, he served as president of the Italian chapter of Doctors Without Borders. When the group won the Nobel Peace Prize that year, he was one of the members who accepted the prize in Oslo, Norway.

Dr. Urbani was one of the doctors who first treated Johnny Chen, the SARS index patient for Vietnam. Because of his years of experience, he quickly recognized that Chen was suffering from a new, highly infectious disease. He immediately began taking extra precautions, isolating SARS patients from the rest of the hospital and requiring all doctors to wear high-filter face masks. On March 5, he requested assistance from the WHO. This resulted in a meeting on March 9 with the health minister of Vietnam, who approved the quarantining of French Hospital. Without Dr. Urbani's experience and contacts with the Vietnam government, the Hanoi outbreak could not have been contained.

Dr. Urbani would not live to see the results of his work, however. On March 11, while flying to Thailand to help combat an outbreak of SARS there, he began to feel sick. He had contracted SARS. On March 29, 2003, Dr. Urbani died in Bangkok, Thailand. He was forty-six years old.

The Amoy Gardens Outbreak

Despite the evolving precautions taken by the health care authorities in Hong Kong, such as banning the use of nebulizers, officials were powerless to stop what was the single worst outbreak of SARS in Asia: the Amoy Gardens outbreak.

Amoy Gardens is a large housing complex of nineteen thirty-story buildings in the Kwun Tong District, a densely populated part of Kowloon. One building, Block E, was particularly hit hard: Of the 329 people who came down with SARS in Amoy Gardens, 130 lived in Block E.

One of the residents of Block E had a thirty-three-year-old brother who lived in Shenzen, just north of Hong Kong. This brother had kidney disease and was receiving twice-weekly treatments at Prince of Wales Hospital. When he came to Hong Kong for his treatments, he stayed at Amoy Gardens, in his brother's twelfth-floor apartment.

The patient had come to Hong Kong on March 14, 2003, and was already ill with the first stages of SARS. He visited Prince of Wales Hospital and had to be admitted because he had pneumonia. His condition improved, however, and he returned to Amoy Gardens on March 19. Three days later, when he returned to Prince of Wales Hospital for his kidney treatment, he again had to be admitted for pneumonia. A test for SARS now existed, and it confirmed that he had the new disease.

By this point, however, he had already infected many people in the Amoy Gardens complex. The infection spread rapidly throughout the building, some five floors above and below the twelfth-floor apartment. Strangely, it seemed to move both upward and downward through the building, which puzzled researchers.

It is now believed that the waste of people who are infected with the virus can spread SARS. Because the plumbing in the Amoy Gardens building was old and the toilet pipes had decayed, the

Officials from the Chinese Food and Environmental Hygiene Department wear protective gear as they gather samples from the Amoy Gardens apartment complex.

virus was able to spread from the bathrooms of people with the disease into the plumbing system of the buildings. Further analysis suggested that exhaust fans in bathrooms and kitchens in the apartment complex helped SARS spread. Microscopic water droplets containing the virus became airborne and were pulled into the apartments through traps in floor drains.

As panic over the disease increased, people began to move out of Amoy Gardens. This caused the disease to spread into the general population of the city, fueled by its relatively long incubation period (the time between infection and showing symptoms of the disease, which was about ten days). On March 31, the government isolated Block E of Amoy Gardens. No one was allowed into or out of the building for the next ten days.

Medical staff help a tenant of Amoy Gardens reenter the complex in April 2003 after being kept in quarantine.

By then, SARS was not only ravaging Hong Kong, but had broken out in several places around the world. At the beginning of April 2003, a new worldwide epidemic had emerged, and scientists were racing to understand the disease.

3

THE SEARCH FOR THE KILLER

Although the SARS virus spread rapidly, bringing Hong Kong almost to its knees in less than a month, the world responded quickly to the threat. The global fight against SARS was remarkable for how quickly the disease was identified and treated. Ultimately, scientists helped to stop the outbreak of SARS around the world; tragically, however, thousands of people became sick and hundreds died before it ended.

Even before the Hong Kong outbreak, scientists were aware of a new disease from Southeast Asia. As we have seen, the early reports of a mysterious outbreak in Guangdong Province had caused the WHO to issue a global alert about avian flu. By the time Dr. Liu Jianlun arrived in

Masked mourners fold a Hong Kong flag over the casket of Lau Kam-yung, a twenty-seven-year-old health-care worker who died of SARS in May 2003. Lau was given a special burial at Gallant Gardens, which is reserved for those who die while performing their duties with exceptional courage.

Hong Kong, however, doctors in Southeast Asia were already trying to learn more about what was suddenly causing such severe cases of pneumonia.

On February 21, the same day that Dr. Liu set out for Hong Kong, an American businessman who lived in Shanghai, Johnny Chen, was staying at the Hotel Metropole. At some point during the next two days, he must have contacted Dr. Liu or one of the people he infected.

On February 23, Chen arrived in Hanoi, the capital of Vietnam, on business. By February 26, he was feeling sick, and on February 28, he was admitted to French Hospital in Hanoi. Recognizing that the man was suffering from a new, extremely dangerous respiratory disease, Dr. Carlo Urbani sent the WHO an emergency letter describing the SARS symptoms on March 5. This was the first time that SARS had been identified as a new disease, and the first time it had been described outside of China. It was also the first time that the disease was called SARS. But it was too late to stop the spread of SARS in Vietnam—Chen had already infected at least twenty-two hospital workers.

Chen's condition continued to worsen, and his doctors decided to transfer him to a more advanced hospital outside of Vietnam—Princess Margaret Hospital in Hong Kong. He died there on March 13, while the SARS epidemic exploded across Hong Kong.

Meanwhile, scientists and physicians around the world scrambled to find ways to combat the epidemic. Their first priority was to find a way to contain SARS and prevent it from spreading. But it was just as important to determine what caused the disease. Knowing the cause would help scientists find ways to prevent further spreading or even to cure those who were already sick.

In Hong Kong, panic developed, and the government had to respond in ways that kept people calm while trying to contain the spread of disease.

Containing SARS

Even before the quarantine of the Amoy Gardens apartment building, Hong Kong had closed all the public schools in the region. The government issued health advice on television and the radio, trying to educate the public about how they could help prevent SARS from spreading. Visiting privileges to most hospitals in Hong Kong were also suspended, and people with the disease were ordered to remain home. On April 11, the government of Hong Kong began to test all passengers on planes departing from Hong Kong to help prevent the spread of the disease to other parts of the world. Although SARS continued to spread throughout hospitals during April, infecting both hospital staff and non-SARS patients, by the end of the month it had slowed. The danger, however, remained. Hong Kong was not removed from the WHO's list of infected areas until June 23, 2003.

Workers spray disinfectant over a classroom to help fight against the spread of SARS in China's Fujian Province in April 2003.

Scientists had greater success in controlling the Vietnam outbreak. The rapid spread of the disease among the health care workers at Hanoi French Hospital convinced them to take drastic steps. First, all non-SARS cases were removed from French Hospital, and it was closed to new admissions. Meanwhile, the Institute of Clinical Research in Tropical Medicine at Bach Mai Hospital was established as a SARS hospital. On March 28, just before the quarantine of Amoy Gardens in Hong Kong, most of the SARS patients from French Hospital were transferred to Bach Mai. The majority of these people were hospital staff. Only two small community outbreaks were tracked by WHO teams to visitors and patients of Hanoi French Hospital.

By separating SARS patients from other patients and taking other precautions, the WHO teams were able to stop the spread of the disease. The Vietnam outbreak lasted only forty-three days. On April 28, the WHO removed the country from its global tourism advisory. Remarkably, none of the workers at Bach Mai Hospital was infected with SARS.

The steps taken in Vietnam proved that if doctors worked quickly enough, a SARS outbreak could be contained. But without a greater understanding of the causes of the disease, it would be impossible to be truly safe from it. Early in the course of the outbreak,

Guangdong Province, somehow, the virus had mutated into a new and deadly form, capable of causing severe pneumonia in human beings: the SARS virus.

The SARS virus is spread by the drops of water, saliva, or mucus that are sprayed in the air when a person who is infected with the disease coughs, sneezes, or cries. The virus can also survive in an infected person's waste. Since diarrhea is often one of the symptoms of SARS, the disease can spread through faulty sewage systems, such as the one in Amoy Gardens.

One troubling aspect of the spread of SARS was that some people seemed to infect many others. Dr. Liu Jianlun, for example, infected several people in the Metropole Hotel. It is not known for sure if there is any medical reason for "superspreading"; some scientists believe that people may not show symptoms early in the course of the disease, allowing them to come into contact with others before they feel sick. Other people believe that some people have more severe symptoms, coughing and spreading the virus more than average. Still others believe that the superspreaders have a higher concentration of the virus in their body. Fear of these superspreaders swept cities around the world during the early days of the global outbreak.

On April 16, only one month after having been created, the WHO's SARS laboratory network announced it had isolated the SARS virus and definitely proved that it was the cause of the new disease. During the course of its research, it had also created a way to test people for SARS.

However, the SARS outbreak was not over yet. It was raging across Southeast Asia, in Hong Kong, Singapore, Taiwan, and China—and now, carried by international jets to the far corners of the world, an outbreak had started in the heart of North America.

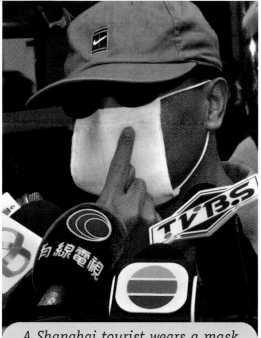

A Shanghai tourist wears a mask while he is interviewed by reporters in Hong Kong in March 2003.

4

THE GLOBAL OUTBREAK

On February 21, 2003, Sui-chu Kwan stepped into an elevator in her hotel. A seventy-eight-year-old grandmother, she and her husband were visiting her son who lived in Hong Kong.

The ride in the elevator proved to be fatal. Kwan Sui-chu was staying at the Metropole Hotel. One of the people who rode the elevator with her that day was Dr. Liu Jianlun.

Two weeks later, Kwan Sui-chu was dead. Doctors in Toronto, Canada, where she and her husband lived, thought at first that she had died of a heart attack; since she had a host of health problems, her death was not thought suspicious. But soon her son, Tse Chi Kwai, became ill with a severe case of pneumonia. He died on March

13. Soon the familiar infection pattern emerged. Health care workers at the hospital that treated Tse, and patients who had come in contact with him, rapidly became ill.

SARS in Canada

On March 26, the government of Canada's province of Ontario declared a public health emergency in Toronto. Thousands of people who might have been exposed to SARS were quarantined in their homes. Some schools were closed. Many hospitals closed their doors to all visitors. Even blood donations by people who had recently visited Southeast Asia were prohibited from entering the Canadian blood supply.

Although the death toll never became as high as it had in Hong Kong, the Canadian outbreak was a major threat. In the heart of North America, in one of the most advanced nations in the world, SARS seemed just as unstoppable as it had been in the villages of Guangdong.

On April 23, the WHO issued a travel advisory for Toronto. The mayor of Toronto angrily demanded that the WHO remove the ban, claiming that the SARS outbreak was under control. Although the travel ban was lifted on April 29, less than a month later, a second

At one point, the Chinese government threatened to imprison for life—or even execute—anyone who broke the SARS quarantine rules. China was also one of the last countries to be removed from the WHO's travel advisory list.

By the end of May, the number of new SARS cases was falling throughout the world. Even with the second outbreaks in Toronto and Taiwan, it was clear that the epidemic was ending. On July 5, Taiwan was removed from the WHO's list of infected countries. The global outbreak was over, but the battle against SARS continues.

Conclusion

By January 2004, SARS had infected 8,422 people around the world and killed 916 of them. The death rate from SARS is at least 10 percent; in elderly people, it may be as high as 50 percent. The SARS epidemic was a worldwide health crisis of a magnitude not seen since the Spanish flu of 1918 to 1920.

Many lessons have been learned from the SARS crisis. The most important of these is the importance of communication among health care officials around the world. Thanks to the efforts of the WHO in coordinating the work of scientists around the world, the SARS virus was identified in only one

The civet cat is not a cat; it is a relative of the mongoose. It lives throughout hot regions of Africa, Asia, and Europe, but prefers tropical rain forests. Civet cats have brown or gray fur, with stripes down the back and sides, with long noses and tails. They range from 17 to 28 inches (43 to 71 centimeters) long and usually weigh from 3 to 10 pounds (1.4 to 4.5 kilograms).

A civet cat can emit a strong odor called musk from glands near its tail. This musk has been used as an ingredient in perfumes and colognes.

Civet cats are considered endangered animals. Despite this, they continue to be hunted for their meat in regions around the world, including Guangdong Province in China. Because of the possible link between civet cats and SARS, in January 2004, the Chinese government ordered the slaughter of 10,000 civet cats.

month; it took decades to identify the influenza virus. Another lesson is the need for openness when a new infection is first discovered. China's attempts to cover up the Guangdong outbreak led to the deadly Hong Kong outbreak. Dr. Urbani's openness, in contrast, allowed Vietnam to contain SARS in less than two months.

In 2004, several new and exciting discoveries regarding SARS were made. A possible animal source for the SARS virus, the civet cat, has now been identified.

A customer browses books on SARS in Shanghai in March 2003. At the time, the Chinese Health Ministry estimated the total numbers of SARS infections in China at 4,698, with a death toll of 224.

Long a delicacy in Guangdong Province, scientists now believe that the disease may have been carried by animals that were killed for food and somehow spread to humans. Although not fully proven, this theory has begun to gain widespread acceptance.

In addition, researchers from Hong Kong and the United States made headlines in September 2004 with claims that they have found chemicals that will stop SARS from spreading. Also, two new vaccines for SARS are currently being tested. If successful, they will prevent healthy people from catching the disease and may help treat people who have already caught SARS. The Chinese are developing the first vaccine. It uses a

THE CENTERS FOR DISEASE CONTROL AND PREVENTION

Part of the United States Public Health Services, the Centers for Disease Control and Prevention (CDC) is one of the most respected organizations fighting infectious diseases in the world. The CDC's mission is to prevent, research, and cure diseases around the world.

Founded in 1946 as the Communicable Disease Center in Atlanta, Georgia, the CDC has led the fight in eradicating diseases. In 1955, it created the Polio Surveillance Unit; by 1991, the disease had almost been completely eradicated in the Western Hemisphere. The CDC's doctors were the leaders of the fight against smallpox in the 1960s, sharing in the triumph of destroying one of humankind's deadliest plagues.

The CDC also researches new diseases. In 1981, it was the first agency to describe cases of AIDS. It has been the first agency to respond to new threats such as the hantavirus outbreak in the western United States in 1993 and the influenza outbreak in Hong Kong in 1997. The CDC's labs helped identify the SARS virus in 2003, and mapped its entire genetic structure within a month of discovering the virus—a remarkable feat of medical detective work.

In 1992, the CDC added the word "prevention" to its name and made preventing diseases a part of its mission. It has helped identify such issues as the link between aspirin and Reye's syndrome, as well as educating the public on the dangers of smoking, drinking, and obesity.

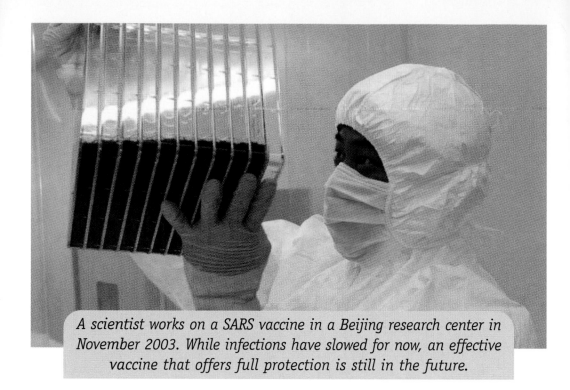

A scientist works on a SARS vaccine in a Beijing research center in November 2003. While infections have slowed for now, an effective vaccine that offers full protection is still in the future.

very traditional method of creating a vaccine: a "killed" virus, one that is not capable of infecting people, is given to a person without SARS. The person's immune system learns how to recognize the disease, thus giving the body a natural defense against SARS. The second vaccine, being developed by the United States National Institute of Allergy and Infectious Diseases (NIAID), has been created using DNA from the SARS virus. The U.S. Centers for Disease Control and Prevention has also been working toward a greater understanding of the disease.

In March 2004, the NIAID vaccine was tested on laboratory mice in a controlled experiment and was effective against exposure to SARS. This vaccine triggers cells to make specific proteins in mice that will hopefully help future scientists create a similar vaccine for humans that would increase their immunity against SARS. According to NIAID scientist Dr. Gary J. Nabel, the new vaccine "dramatically reduced the level of the virus in the lungs of infected mice more than a millionfold." The U.S. Centers for Disease Control and Prevention has also been working toward a greater understanding of the disease.

Still another scientific discovery regarding SARS was newsworthy in 2004. At that time, doctors in Singapore suspected that the deadly respiratory illness could be detected in human tears. After they swabbed the tear ducts of thirty-six patients suspected of having SARS, eight were found to positively have the illness, even though it was in its earliest stages and the patients were experiencing few symptoms. The discovery is significant because it now means that SARS can be detected earlier and more easily. Scientists are also looking at ways in which SARS might have spread by contact with human tears.

But SARS continues to infect people. Two new cases were reported in Guangdong in January 2004. Neither led to another outbreak, but the world must remain prepared for another epidemic. The lessons learned

A baby is examined at Ben Gurion Airport in Israel after arriving from Toronto in April 2003. Although inconvenient, inspecting or even banning travelers from infected countries is sometimes necessary to prevent the spread of epidemics.

from combating the SARS epidemic must be used to fight the next outbreak—whether it is SARS, influenza, or a new disease. "We're living in [an] age of . . . emerging health threats," said Dr. Julie Gerberding, director of the Centers for Disease Control and Prevention on CNN. "If it's not SARS, it will be something else."

GLOSSARY

acquired immunodeficiency syndrome (AIDS)
A disease of the immune system that is spread through direct contact with bodily fluids such as blood and semen or through blood transfusions. It cannot be spread by everyday human contact such as hugging or kissing. The virus associated with AIDS is called HIV.

acute Reaching a crisis rapidly, or extremely severe.

antibiotic A substance largely derived from a microorganism that is given to a patient by his or her doctor to help kill bacteria in the person's system.

bacteria Single-celled organisms that live in soil, water, organic matter, and the bodies of plants and animals.

chlamydia A disease or infection caused by the chlamydia bacterium. When SARS first appeared, scientists believed it was linked to this bacterium, but they were proven wrong.

deoxyribonucleic acid (DNA) Double-stranded polynucleotide formed from two separate chains of deoxyribonucleotide units; serves as the carrier of genetic information.

Ebola An RNA virus of African origin that causes an often fatal hemorrhagic fever and for which there is no known cure.

epidemiologist A medical scientist who studies the occurrence of disease or events related to disease outbreaks in specific populations.

hantavirus An RNA virus that is transmitted by rodent feces and urine; it causes acute respiratory illness and hemorrhagic fever and is marked by kidney failure.

immune system The body's main defense against disease.

index patient The first person in a region to get a new disease.

influenza An acute, highly contagious disease caused by various RNA viruses and characterized by fever, severe aches and pains, and inflammation of the mucous membranes.

pneumonia An acute or chronic disease marked by inflammation of the lungs and caused by viruses, bacteria, and chemical agents.

quarantine A period during which someone suspected of carrying a contagious disease is kept in confinement.

ribonucleic acid (RNA) A chemical found in the nucleus and cytoplasm of cells that plays a significant role in protein synthesis; its structure is similar to that of DNA.

superspreader One person with an illness that is thought to spread that illness to many people, thereby creating an outbreak.

tuberculosis A highly communicable disease caused by a mycobacterium that adversely affects the lungs.

vaccine An injection of a substance that is given to make the body produce defense mechanisms against a certain disease.

virus Infectious particle consisting of nucleic acid (RNA or DNA) enclosed in a protein coat.

World Health Organization (WHO) A global health agency created in 1948 by the United Nations and formed with members from 192 nations around the world.

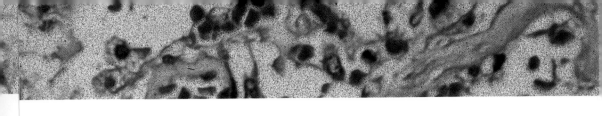

INDEX

CREDITS

About the Author

Fred Ramen is a writer and computer programmer who is the author of fourteen books for the Rosen Publishing Group. His interests include military history, science fiction, and French cuisine. Mr. Ramen lives in New York City.

Photo Credits